Modern Ice Cream Recipes

by

Earl Goldman

A Nitty Gritty Book*
Published by
Nitty Gritty Productions
P.O. Box 2008
Benicia. California 94510

*Nitty Gritty Books - Trademark
Owned by Nitty Gritty Productions
Benicia. California

ISBN 0-911954-82-1

Make healthy & delicious ice cream the easy way with Modern Ice Cream Recipes

- Simple instructions for all ice cream makers from hand crank models to modern "no ice/no salt" electrics.

- Separate ingredients for quarts & gallons for every recipe.

- Twelve basic vanilla recipes can each be used with 45 flavor additives for over 500 combinations.

- An added bonus of sherbets, sauces, toppings & ice cream cakes & pies.

TABLE OF CONTENTS

INTRODUCTION

The first ice cream was created by Jacques, a French chef to the court of Charles I of England in 1640.

Soon afterward it was made in Paris and in the year 1660 an Italian cook named Procopio Cultelli from Palermo established his "Cafe Procope," where for the first time ice cream was made available to the common man. This practice soon spread to other Parisian eateries.

Ice cream was introduced next to England from France by Carlo Gatti and was served at the court of King Charles I. The earliest printed record of cream ices is found in "The Experienced English Housekeeper," by Elizabeth Raffald, published in the year 1769. Ice cream made its way to the New World not long after.

The first ice cream parlor in America was owned and operated by an imaginative man named Hall in New York. He was soon copied by many others and ice cream parlors sprang up throughout New York City. George

Continued

Washington was so delighted with the ice cream he tasted at Mr. Hall's establishment that he later bought a "cream machine for making ice."

In fact, ice cream seems to have been a favorite of many of our founding fathers. Thomas Jefferson learned recipes while he was in France. He served Meringue Glacee and Baked Alaska at many of his state dinners.

Ice cream might not have been so popular among our early statesmen had they not had servants to prepare it for them. The process was time-consuming and quite tiring. It demanded great perseverance and patience, for none of the equipment was mechanized. The ingredients were placed in a metal container which was then placed in a wooden bucket filled with ice. These ingredients then had to be beaten by hand until the ice cream solidified. In 1846 an American woman named Nancy Johnson invented an ice cream freezer with a rotary element called a "dasher." It was connected to an outside handle. As this handle was rotated it caused the

dasher to whip the ingredients, which kept them creamy and smooth during the freezing process. The present day home ice cream freezer, whether hand-cranked or electric, operates on this same principle.

With the help of this book, you will be able to make at home ice creams and sherbets of superior quality and flavor to delight your family and friends. And, you will be able to save money as well. Homemade ice creams and sherbets always cost less than their store-bought counterparts if the comparison is made by weight. (Normally the homemade product weighs at least twice as much simply because it contains less air.) A third and most important advantage is that making ice cream at home is a great deal of fun!

TYPES OF "ICE CREAM"

There are many different types of "ice cream." In general, ice cream is a frozen cream and milk product with sweetening and flavorings added. There are, however, many variations on this product.

Ice milk is a product similar to ice cream but it contains less milk fat and total milk solids. It is often sold in its soft state at roadside refreshment stands under the name of "frostie" or "softie."

Frozen custard or French ice cream is a frozen product in which eggs or egg yolks are added to the usual ice cream ingredients to make a richer result.

Sherbet is made of milk or milk and cream. Sweeteners, fruit or fruit juices, water, flavorings, and stabilizers may also be added. The number of calories is slightly less than that contained by ice cream. Sherbets have twice the amount of sugar as ice cream.

Mousse is a frozen dessert made of sweetened, flavored whipped cream or thin cream and gelatine.

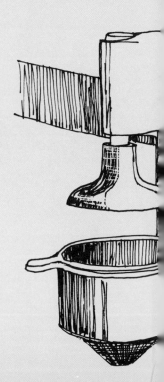

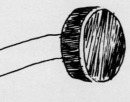

Fruit ices are made by using fruit, fruit juices, water and sweeteners — no milk. Many of the flavorings that are used for sherbet are also added.

Mellorine or diet or imitation ice cream is a frozen dessert made with vegetable fats such as cottonseed or soybean oil, rather than with milk fats. Since vegetable fats do not require refrigeration for storage, mellorine is less expensive to produce than ice cream made with milk fats. Sale is regulated by state laws and permitted in only 14 states.

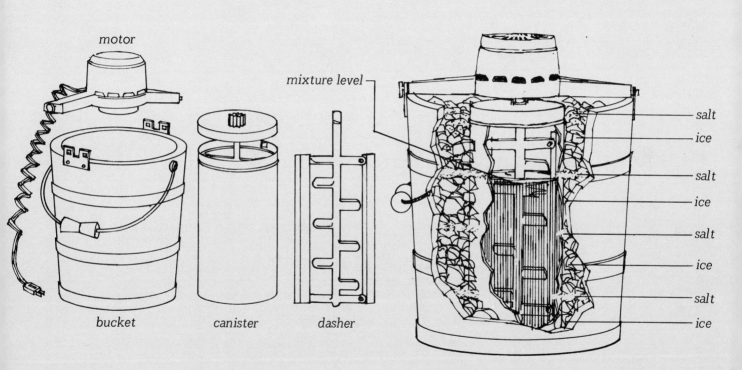

motor

bucket

canister

dasher

mixture level

salt
ice
salt
ice
salt
ice
salt
ice

SELECTING AN OLD FASHIONED FREEZER

Old fashioned ice cream freezers are a fairly standard product. The typical maker consists of a two gallon bucket made of wood, plastic, or fiberglass into which a one gallon ice cream canister is placed. The canister contains a dasher which remains still while the canister turns. The wooden bucket is the old standard, as it is probably the most durable. However, it has one major drawback. It must be soaked in water for several hours before use so that the staves will swell, otherwise it will leak like a sieve.

The regular plastic bucket is acceptable; however, it is not particularly durable, and is relatively poorly insulated.

Fiberglass is extremely strong and long lasting, and if it is reasonably thick, it should prove to be both durable and a good insulating material.

The Waring freezer makes approximately one quart, and is much smaller, however it works fine, and is a sensible choice for those who make small quantities.

Continued

The canisters are similar in most freezers. The ones with the see-through plastic covers are particularly nice, because they allow the user to see the mix harden.

Electric mixers are easier to use than hand cranked models and are well worth their added cost; however, one drawback is that they cannot be used for camp-outs and picnics where there is no electricity. The hand crank models are also fun for the kids, although most modern day children soon tire of cranking.

As is true with most products with a long useful life, the reader would be advised well to spend a little more and get the highest quality model that his budget will allow.

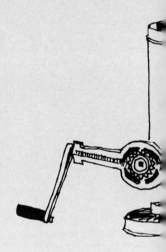

OLD FASHIONED FREEZER INSTRUCTIONS

Whether you are using an old fashioned electric or hand cranked model, the following instructions should produce consistent results when making ice cream or sherbet:

1. It is advisable to scald the inner canister and beaters with boiling water, however hot water from the tap will do if boiling water is not available. Simply pour boiling water into the canister with the dasher in place, and then pour it off.
2. Pour the chilled mixture through a fine mesh strainer into the canister, using a wooden spoon to force the mixture through the mesh. Or, if you prefer, you may use your blender or food processor to smooth the chilled mixture. Place the canister in the refrigerator to chill overnight if desired—although not really necessary, this helps make a smoother ice cream.

Continued

3. After chilling the mixture, place the dasher in the canister, put the cover in place, and place the canister in the bucket. If the bucket is made of wood, it should have been soaked in water for several hours, or overnight so that its wooden sides will expand to prevent leakage. This is, of course, unnecessary with plastic or fiberglass buckets.

4. Ice should be chopped up into small coarse pieces. One can buy crushed ice, use an ice crusher (coarse setting), or simply place large pieces in an old burlap bag, or pillow case, and use a hammer to crush them. The smaller the pieces, the more actual ice (by weight) you will be able to put in the bucket. However, because small pieces have more surface area than large pieces, they will melt faster. So adjust the size to your particular needs. Always have plenty of ice on hand. It usually requires 25 lbs. of ice to make a gallon of ice cream. While you are at it, you can make two 1-gallon batches with the same amount of ice.

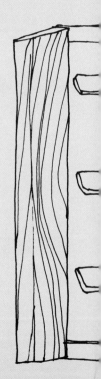

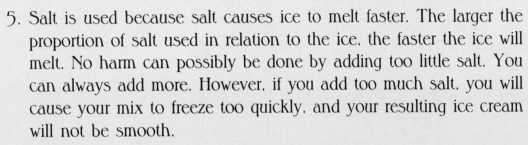

5. Salt is used because salt causes ice to melt faster. The larger the proportion of salt used in relation to the ice, the faster the ice will melt. No harm can possibly be done by adding too little salt. You can always add more. However, if you add too much salt, you will cause your mix to freeze too quickly, and your resulting ice cream will not be smooth.

Simply place about three inches of crushed ice in the bucket with the canister in place, then add about two handfuls of salt. Then add three more inches of ice, then two more handfuls of salt. When the ice salt mixture is just below the top of the canister, you can plug in the electric mixer, or start cranking the hand operated one.

6. Keep cranking steadily until the mixture thickens. With a hand operated model, keep cranking until you can't crank any longer. With an electric model, pull the plug when the motor starts to labor. If the mixture

Continued

does not thicken after 20 minutes, just pour off some of the water through the drain hole and then add two or three more handfuls of salt and another layer of ice.

7. Remove the canister from the bucket and wipe the outside of the canister dry with a towel to remove all traces of salt. Remove the dasher and sample your luscious frozen delicacy. Then place several layers of wax paper over the ice cream. Replace the canister cover and place the canister back into the bucket. Pour the excess water off and add sufficient layers of ice and salt to fill the bucket. Place a stack of newspapers on top for insulation and set ice cream aside to cure for at least three hours. If you have a good home freezer that maintains a temperature of 0° or thereabouts, you can remove the ice cream from the canister immediately, place it in freezer containers, and let it cure for several hours in your home freezer. You can then make additional batches of ice cream or sherbet in your ice cream freezer.

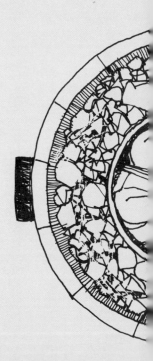

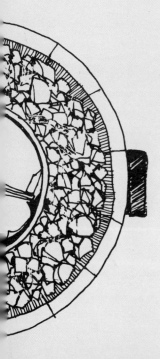

Remember that on hot days, freezers do not work as efficiently as you might think. 0 degrees is not often attained by home quality electric refrigerator-freezers. However, the old fashioned method is simple and it always works.

8. After you and your guests have had your fill, you can spoon the extra ice cream into freezer containers for storage. Don't be surprised if the ice cream gets extremely hard in your freezer and has to be softened before being served. This is a characteristic of the homemade product, as it is very dense. One quart of homemade ice cream weighs about the same as two quarts of commercial ice cream.

SELECTION OF A MODERN FREEZER

Modern, all electric ice cream freezers are extremely easy to use because they do not require ice and salt.

The Simac and Minigel are two brands which are available in many houseware and gourmet shops. They contain electric freezers which make from one to one and one half quarts in less than 30 minutes.

They allow lovers of home made ice cream to start the freezer during dinner and enjoy freshly made ice cream for dessert with a minimum of effort and clean up.

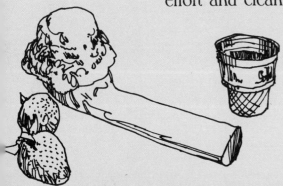

MODERN FREEZER INSTRUCTIONS

Modern all electric ice cream freezers do not require ice and salt, therefore, they are easier to use. Instructions are as follows:

1. Place agitator in bowl of freezer.
2. Turn on the chill switch and let the machine chill for five minutes.
3. If your mixture is not perfectly smooth, remove lumps by pouring the chilled mixture through a fine mesh strainer into the freezer bowl, using a wooden spoon to force the mixture through the mesh. Or, if you prefer, use your blender or food processor to smooth the chilled mixture.
4. Place cover on bowl and turn on the churn switch.
5. Set timer for 20 minutes. You can take the cover off while the machine is running and test the results with a small spoon. Keep resetting timer for more time so that the mixture keeps churning until it is so hard that the entire mix clings to the agitator and rotates with it.

6. Remove ice cream from freezer and serve at once, or place in freezer container and store in your refrigerator's freezer section, or your home freezer. It is not desirable to leave it in the ice cream maker as it will get too hard to remove easily.

Clean up is easy. If your freezer bowl is removable, wash it as you would any other stainless steel bowl. If it is fixed in place, pour a cup of hot water into the bowl and wash with a sponge. Use the sponge to remove the water from the bowl, and then repeat the process. Finally wipe dry with a kitchen towel.

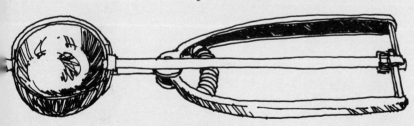

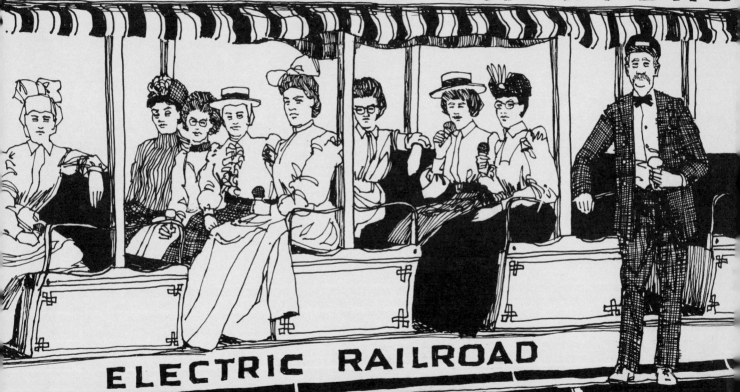

ICE CUBE TRAY METHOD

All of the recipes in this book may be made in the ice cube trays of your refrigerator. However, the results will not be as smooth, and the use of an ice cream freezer is strongly recommended.

If you do not have one, simply make one-fourth of the recipe called for, and freeze it in your ice cube trays until it is mushy. Then remove the partially frozen mix from the trays and beat it with an electric mixer until it is smooth. Then pour it back into the trays and freeze until solid. It is practically impossible to avoid crystals from forming; however, many people find this method satisfactory.

RECIPE INFORMATION

All of the recipes in this book are designed to make either four quarts or one quart of ice cream or sherbet. Because ice cream increases in volume during the freezing process, due to air which is whipped into it by the dasher, one gallon freezer canisters should be filled only three-fourths full. Four versions of each of the basic vanilla recipes are provided. The two large ones will fill the canisters to three fourths full and should be used if a gallon or quart of vanilla ice cream is desired. The small version allows for the addition of fruit or other flavoring ingredients without overfilling the canister.

Once you have tried a particular recipe, make a note on the page as to your personal taste to guide you in the amount of flavoring and sugar to use the next time you make it.

Do not judge the taste of the ice cream by the taste of the mix before freezing. The mix will always taste overly sweet and flavorful before it is frozen.

RECIPE INFORMATION Continued

A recipe for delicious, sugar-free ice cream made with half-and-half and an artificial sweetener is given on page 32. If a sugar-free, lower calorie ice milk is preferred use milk instead of half-and-half. For those not watching calories, a richer version can be made by substituting whipping cream for part of the half-and-half. For an extra smooth texture, save one cup of cream to be whipped and folded into the custard along with the egg whites just before freezing.

Using any version of this sugar-free recipe as the base, different flavors can be made provided the ingredients used are sugar-free or artificially sweetened. Many of the flavorful recipes in the sherbet section (page 75) make tasty, low calorie desserts when an artificial sweetener is used. Or, if you are a calorie watcher who can have sugar, try the rich-tasting ice milk on page 33.

Please remember that sugar helps frozen desserts to keep better and those made without sugar are best eaten within a few days.

VANILLA RECIPES ARE BASIC

The following eleven vanilla recipes vary from ultra-rich catering quality ice cream using eggs and cream to inexpensive ice milk made with evaporated milk. They form the basic ingredient for all of the flavored ice cream recipes which follow. Each has a large and small version.

First select the vanilla recipe that suits the occasion (and your pocketbook). Then choose a flavor from the section on flavored ice creams. This way, you have a choice of many different qualities of ice cream for whatever flavor you select. **If you are adding fruit or an ingredient that will increase the volume of the basic vanilla, use the smaller recipe. If you want plain, delicious vanilla, use the larger recipe.**

An easy way to have a variety of flavors is to divide a gallon of vanilla ice cream into thirds and add a different flavor to each third. Pack into containers and store in the freezer.

VANILLA CUSTARD ICE CREAM

Large				**Small**		
Quart		Gallon		Quart		Gallon
1 ½	cups whole milk	6		1 ⅓	cups whole milk	5 ¼
3	egg yolks	12		2	egg yolks	9
¼	tsp. salt	1		¼	tsp. salt	¾
⅔	cups sugar	2 ¼		¼	cups sugar	1 ⅞
1	T. vanilla extract	4		¾	T. vanilla extract	3
1	cups whipping cream	4		¾	cups whipping cream	3

Heat milk in large saucepan to boiling point. Add sugar and stir until dissolved. In large bowl beat together egg yolks and salt. Slowly stir about half of the scalded milk mixture into egg yolks. Return egg yolk mixture to milk in saucepan. Cook over medium heat, stirring constantly, until mixture thickens slightly and coats back of spoon. Remove from heat at once. Pour through strainer into freezer canister. Chill thoroughly. Just before freezing, stir in vanilla and cream.

VANILLA CUSTARD ICE CREAM Continued

This is a delicious catering quality custard ice cream. Please notice that it uses a ratio of approximately 1½ parts milk to 1 part cream. By substituting additional cream for some of the milk, it can be made even richer.

You will have lots of leftover egg whites. Use them for making Baked Alaska (page 134), sherbet (page 75) or Meringue Ice Cream Cups (page 132), which are delicious filled with ice cream and topped with fresh berries or peaches.

This is our favorite vanilla.

RICH VANILLA ICE CREAM

Large			**Small**		
Quart		Gallon	Quart		Gallon
1 ½	cups whole milk	6	1	cups whole milk	4
⅔	cups sugar	2 ¼	½	cups sugar	1 ¾
¼	tsp. salt	1	¼	tsp. salt	¾
1	T. vanilla extract	3	½	T. vanilla extract	2
1 ½	cups whipping cream	6	1	cups whipping cream	4

Heat ½ of milk in saucepan until lukewarm. Add sugar and salt. Stir until dissolved. Add remaining milk. Chill thoroughly. Just before freezing add vanilla and cream.

FRENCH VANILLA ICE CREAM

Large			Small		
Quart		Gallon	Quart		Gallon
1	cups whole milk	4	⅔	cups whole milk	2⅔
½	cups sugar	2¼	½	cups sugar	1½
¼	tsp. salt	1	¼	tsp. salt	¾
2	eggs	6	1	eggs	4
1	T. vanilla extract	4	1	T. vanilla extract	3
1½	cups whipping cream	6	1	cups whipping cream	4

Heat ½ of the milk until lukewarm. Add sugar and salt. Stir until dissolved. Beat eggs until fluffy. Blend in milk-sugar mixture. Add remaining milk. Chill thoroughly. When ready to freeze stir in vanilla and cream.

PHILADELPHIA VANILLA ICE CREAM

Large				Small			
Quart			Gallon	Quart			Gallon
½	envelopes unflavored gelatin		1½	¼	envelopes unflavored gelatin		1
1½	cups whole milk		6	1	cups whole milk		4
⅔	cups sugar		2½	½	cups sugar		1⅔
¼	tsp. salt		1	¼	tsp. salt		½
1	T. vanilla extract		4	1	T. vanilla extract		3
1	cups whipping cream		4	¾	cups whipping cream		3

Sprinkle gelatin over ½ cup milk. Set aside. Heat remaining milk until lukewarm. Add softened gelatin, sugar and salt. Stir until dissolved. Stir in remaining milk and chill. Just before freezing add vanilla and cream.

HALF-AND-HALF VANILLA ICE CREAM

	Large			Small	
Quart		Gallon	Quart		Gallon
3	cups half-and-half	12	2	cups half-and-half	8
⅔	cups sugar	2½	½	cups sugar	1⅔
¼	tsp. salt	1	¼	tsp. salt	½
1	T. vanilla extract	4	1	T. vanilla extract	3

Heat half of half-and-half until lukewarm. Add sugar and salt. Stir until dissolved. Stir in remaining half-and-half and chill thoroughly. Add vanilla and freeze.

VANILLA PUDDING ICE CREAM

Large				**Small**			
Quart			Gallon	Quart			Gallon
2	cups whole milk		8	1½	cups whole milk		5½
½	boxes (3 ozs.) vanilla pudding mix		2	¼	boxes (3 ozs.) vanilla pudding mix		1
¼	cup light corn syrup		1	¼	cup light corn syrup		⅔
½	T. vanilla extract		2	½	T. vanilla extract		2
½	cups whipping cream		2	½	cups whipping cream		2

Combine half of milk and all of the pudding mix in saucepan. Cook over medium heat, stirring constantly, until thickened. Stir in corn syrup and remaining milk. Chill. Just before freezing add vanilla and cream.

MARSHMALLOW VANILLA ICE CREAM

Large			Small	
Quart		Gallon	Quart		Gallon
15	regular-size marshmallows	60	10	regular-size marshmallows	40
½	cups sugar	1 ½	¼	cups sugar	1
1 ¾	cups whole milk	7	1 ¼	cups whole milk	5
¼	tsp. salt	1	¼	tsp. salt	½
1	T. vanilla extract	3	½	T. vanilla extract	2
1 ¼	cups whipping cream	5	¾	cups whipping cream	3

Combine marshmallows, sugar and ⅓ of milk in saucepan. Heat, stirring, until marshmallows are melted. Remove from heat and add remaining milk, salt and vanilla, and chill. Just before freezing add cream.

SUGAR-FREE VANILLA ICE CREAM

Large				Small			
Quart			Gallon	Quart			Gallon
¼	envelopes unflavored gelatin		2	½	envelopes unflavored gelatin		1 ½
3	cups half-and-half		12	2	cups half-and-half		8
2	eggs, separated		6	1	eggs, separated		4
¼	tsp. salt		¾	¼	tsp. salt		½
15	packets of nutrasweet		60	10	packets of nutrasweet		40
1 ½	T. vanilla extract		6	1	T. vanilla extract		4

Sprinkle gelatin over ½ cup half-and-half. Set aside. Beat egg yolks, salt and half of half-and-half together in saucepan. Cook, stirring constantly, over medium heat until mixture thickens slightly and coats the back of spoon. Remove from heat at once. Add softened gelatin and stir until dissolved. Blend in remaining half-and-half. Chill. Just before freezing, add nutrasweet and vanilla and beat egg whites until stiff. Fold into custard.

VANILLA CUSTARD ICE MILK

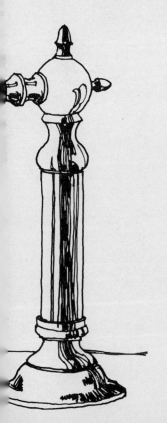

Large			Small		
Quart		Gallon	Quart		Gallon
½	envelopes unflavored gelatin	2	⅓	envelopes unflavored gelatin	1 ½
3	cups whole milk	12	2	cups whole milk	8
2	eggs, separated	6	1	eggs, separated	4
⅔	cups sugar	2 ¼	⅓	cups sugar	1 ½
1	T. vanilla extract	3	¼	T. vanilla extract	2
¼	tsp. salt	1	¼	tsp. salt	½

Sprinkle gelatin over ½ cup milk. Set aside. Beat egg yolks, sugar and salt in saucepan. Stir in remaining milk. Cook, stirring constantly, until mixture thickens slightly and coats back of spoon. Remove from heat at once. Add softened gelatin and stir until dissolved. Add vanilla. Pour into freezer canister and chill. Just before freezing beat egg whites until stiff. Fold into custard.

VANILLA EVAPORATED ICE MILK

	Large			Small	
Quart		Gallon	Quart		Gallon
⅔	cups sugar	2½	⅓	cups sugar	1⅓
¼	tsp. salt	½	¼	tsp. salt	¼
1	T. flour	4	½	T. flour	2
1⅔	cups evaporated milk	6⅔	1¼	cups evaporated milk	5
½	cups water	2	⅓	cups water	1⅓
1	eggs	4	1	eggs	3
1	T. vanilla extract	3	½	T. vanilla extract	2

Combine sugar, salt and flour in saucepan. Add 1 cup evaporated milk and the water. Cook, stirring frequently, until mixture is slightly thickened. Beat eggs. Stir a small portion of the mixture into eggs. Return to mixture in pan. Cook 2 minutes, stirring constantly. Remove from heat. Add vanilla and remaining evaporated milk. Chill thoroughly. Freeze.

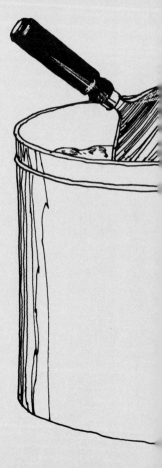

VANILLA FROZEN YOGURT

	Large			**Small**	
Quart		Gallon	Quart		Gallon
⅓	envelopes unflavored gelatin	1 ½	¼	envelopes unflavored gelatin	1
⅔	quarts plain yogurt	2½	½	quarts plain yogurt	2
1	eggs, separated	5	1	eggs, separated	4
⅔	cups sugar	2½	½	cups sugar	2
1 ¼	T. vanilla extract	5	1	T. vanilla extract	4
¼	tsp. salt	¾	¼	tsp. salt	½

Sprinkle gelatin over ¼ cup cold water in small saucepan. Place over very low heat. Stir until gelatin dissolves. Remove from heat. In large mixing bowl beat yogurt, egg yolks, half of sugar, vanilla and salt together well. Stir some of yogurt mixture into gelatin. Return to mixing bowl and beat until blended. Beat egg whites until frothy. Gradually add remaining sugar and beat until a stiff meringue is formed. Fold meringue into yogurt mixture, and chill thoroughly. Freeze.

35

FLAVORED ICE CREAMS

Normally, commercially made vanilla ice creams are slightly richer in butterfat content than their flavored counterparts. This is because the flavorings cost money, and something (the extra butterfat) must be taken out to make up for the added cost of the flavorings.

In making your own ice cream, you are not limited by cost considerations, and you can select a rich, expensive vanilla recipe for your base and have the finest flavored ice cream you've ever experienced.

All of the following flavorings can be used with any of the preceding vanilla recipes.

STRAWBERRIES AND CREAM

Gallon	Quart
2 to 3 baskets ripe strawberries	½ to ⅔ basket ripe strawberries
Sugar	Sugar

A small vanilla recipe from pages 24 through 35

Hull, wash and slice strawberries just before using. Measure and add about 2 tablespoons sugar for each cup of berries. Stir to dissolve sugar. Fold into vanilla ice cream as soon as it is frozen but still soft.

This method keeps the flavor and color of the strawberries and ice cream separate. A wonderful summertime treat.

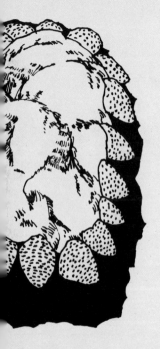

FRESH STRAWBERRY ICE CREAM

Gallon	Quart
2 to 3 baskets ripe strawberries	½ to ⅔ basket ripe strawberries
Sugar	Sugar

A small vanilla recipe from pages 24 through 35

Hull and wash strawberries just before using. Puree in blender, food mill or processor. Measure and add 2 tablespoons sugar for each cup of puree. Stir to dissolve. Add to ice cream mixture just before freezing.

If a darker pink color is desired, add a few drops of red food coloring.

CHOCOLATE ICE CREAM

Gallon	Quart
5 squares unsweetened baking chocolate	1 ¼ squares unsweetened baking chocolate
½ cup sugar	⅛ cup sugar

A large vanilla recipe from pages 24 through 35

Melt chocolate over hot, not boiling, water or in microwave oven. Add melted chocolate and sugar to the warm mixture in ice cream recipe. Stir until well blended. Complete ice cream as recipe directs.

For Bittersweet Chocolate Ice Cream, omit sugar and increase chocolate by 20%.

ROCKY ROAD ICE CREAM

Gallon	Quart
5 squares unsweetened baking chocolate	1 ¼ squares unsweetened baking chocolate
3 cups miniature marshmallows	⅔ cup miniature marshmallows

A small vanilla recipe from pages 24 through 35

Melt chocolate over hot, not boiling, water or in microwave oven. Add melted chocolate to warm mixture in ice cream recipe. Stir until well blended. When ice cream is partially frozen and still soft, stir in marshmallows and continue freezing.

COFFEE ICE CREAM

Gallon | Quart
6 T. instant coffee | ½ T. instant coffee

A large vanilla recipe from pages 24 through 35

Add instant coffee to the warm mixture in ice cream recipe. Add more coffee if a stronger flavor is desired. Remember the flavor will not be quite so strong after the ice cream is frozen.

For Mocha Chip Ice Cream, add a large 12-ounce package for the gallon (or ¼ package for the quart) of miniature semi-sweet chocolate chips after ice cream is frozen but still soft.

CARAMEL ICE CREAM

Sugar in ice cream recipe on pages 24 through 35
1 cup boiling water
A large vanilla recipe from pages 24 through 35

Use the amount of sugar called for in the vanilla recipe you are following. Place half of it in a saucepan over low heat. Stir until sugar melts and is the color of maple sugar. Take care not to let the sugar over-brown as it will give the ice cream a burned flavor. Add boiling water to melted sugar and simmer until it is the consistency of hot syrup. Add remaining half of sugar and stir to dissolve. Use this mixture in place of the sugar in ice cream recipe. Complete ice cream recipe as recipe directs.

PISTACHIO ICE CREAM

Gallon	Quart
½ pound pistachio nuts	⅛ pound pistachio nuts
Green food coloring	Green food coloring

A large vanilla recipe from pages 24 through 35

If the nuts still have their skins, pour boiling water over them. Rinse with cold water and drain. Pinch off the skins and dry nuts on paper towels. Chop finely and add to the ice cream mix just before freezing. Blend in a few drops of food coloring. This is particularly nice for the holiday season.

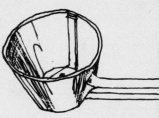

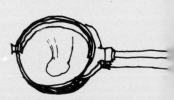

ORANGE ICE CREAM

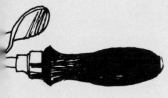

Gallon	Quart
2 cans (6 ounce size) frozen orange juice concentrate	½ can (6 ounce size) frozen orange juice concentrate

A small vanilla recipe from pages 24 through 35

Thaw orange juice concentrate. Add to ice cream mix and stir until well blended. This is preferable to using fresh juice since less water is added and the resulting mixture is richer.

PEPPERMINT STICK ICE CREAM

Gallon	Quart
1 pound peppermint stick candy, finely crushed	¼ pound peppermint stick candy, finely crushed

A small vanilla recipe from pages 24 through 35

Candy may be added to ice cream in two ways. Either soak crushed candy overnight in 2 cups of milk or half-and-half (depending on which is used in the recipe you are using) and then substitute the candy-milk mixture for 2 cups of milk or half-and-half called for in the ice cream recipe; or fold the crushed candy, without soaking it, into the ice cream after it is partially frozen.

TUTTI-FRUTTI ICE CREAM

Gallon	Quart
3 cups assorted dried or candied fruits	¾ cup assorted dried or candied fruits

A small vanilla recipe from pages 24 through 35

Finely chop fruits. If desired, soak for several hours in rum or fruit juice. Drain well and add fruit to ice cream when it is frozen but still soft.

FRESH BLUEBERRY ICE CREAM

Gallon	Quart -
2 baskets fresh blueberries	½ basket fresh blueberries
½ cup sugar	⅛ cup sugar
½ cup water	⅛ cup water

A small vanilla recipe from pages 24 through 35

Wash berries. Simmer with sugar and water until soft. Cool and force through a sieve or food mill, or puree in blender or food processor. Add to ice cream mixture before freezing. Stir until well blended.

BLUEBERRIES AND CREAM

Gallon	Quart
3 baskets fresh blueberries	¾ basket fresh blueberries
Sugar	Sugar

A small vanilla recipe from pages 24 through 35

Wash berries and measure into bowl. Add about 2 tablespoons sugar for each cup of berries. (The exact amount of sugar will depend on personal taste and the tartness of the berries.) Stir and set aside until berries absorb the sugar. Fold sweetened berries into ice cream after it is frozen but still soft.

LEMON OR LIME ICE CREAM

Gallon	Quart
2 cans frozen lemon or lime juice concentrate	½ can frozen lemon or lime juice concentrate

A small vanilla recipe from pages 24 through 35

Thaw juice. Add to ice cream mix and stir until well blended. The use of frozen concentrate is preferable to fresh juice because less water is added and the resulting mixture is richer and the flavor better.

MANGO ICE CREAM

Gallon	Quart
3 cups ripe mango pulp	¾ cup ripe mango pulp

A small vanilla recipe from pages 24 through 35

Add mango pulp to ice cream mixture before freezing. Stir until well blended.

RUM RAISIN ICE CREAM

Gallon	Quart
2 cups seedless raisins	½ cup seedless raisins
6 T. rum	2 T. rum

A small vanilla recipe from pages 24 through 35

Grind or finely chop raisins. Add rum and stir. Allow to stand for several hours. Add to ice cream when frozen but still soft.

For variety, add chopped walnuts or pecans.

This is a nice ice cream for the holiday season.

MOCHA ICE CREAM

Gallon	Quart
1 bag (12 ounces) semi-sweet chocolate chips	¼ bag semi-sweet chocolate chips
6 T. instant coffee	1 ½ T. instant coffee

A small vanilla recipe from pages 24 through 35

Melt chocolate over hot, not boiling, water or in microwave oven. Add instant coffee and stir to blend. Add coffee-chocolate mixture to warm mixture in ice cream recipe. Complete ice cream as recipe directs.

FRESH CHERRY ICE CREAM

Gallon	Quart
3 baskets ripe cherries	¾ basket ripe cherries
Sugar	Sugar
Red food coloring, if desired	Red food coloring, if desired

A small vanilla recipe from pages 24 through 35

Wash, pit and quarter cherries. Measure and add about 2 tablespoons sugar for each cup of cherries. (The exact amount of sugar will depend on personal preference and the tartness of the cherries.) Stir and let stand to dissolve sugar. Add to ice cream when frozen but still soft. If red food coloring is used, add it to the ice cream mix before it is frozen.

FRESH RASPBERRY ICE CREAM

Gallon	Quart
3 baskets ripe raspberries	¾ basket ripe raspberries
Sugar	Sugar

A small vanilla recipe from pages 24 through 35

Crush raspberries and add about 2 tablespoons sugar for each cup of berries. (The exact amount of sugar will depend on sweetness of berries and personal preference.) Stir to dissolve sugar. Add to ice cream mixture just before freezing. Add red food coloring if a pinker color is desired.

RASPBERRIES AND CREAM

Gallon	Quart
3 baskets ripe raspberries	¾ basket ripe raspberries
Sugar	Sugar

A small vanilla recipe from pages 24 through 35

Wash raspberries and add about 2 tablespoons sugar for each cup of berries. (The exact amount of sugar will depend on tartness of berries and personal preference.) Stir to dissolve sugar. Fold sweetened berries into ice cream after it is frozen but still soft.

FRESH PEACH ICE CREAM

Gallon	Quart
4 cups crushed ripe peaches	1 cup crushed ripe peaches
9 T. sugar	2 T. sugar

A small vanilla recipe from pages 24 through 35

Combine peaches and sugar. Stir to dissolve sugar. Add to ice cream mixture before freezing.

FRESH APRICOT RIPPLE ICE CREAM

Gallon	Quart
4 cups crushed ripe apricots	1 cup crushed ripe apricots
9 T. sugar	2 T. sugar

A small vanilla recipe from pages 24 through 35

Combine apricots and sugar. Stir to dissolve. Stir through ice cream when frozen but still soft.

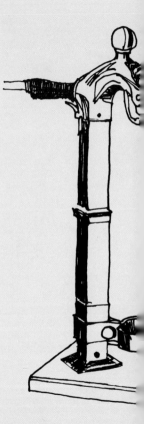

PINEAPPLE ICE CREAM

Gallon	Quart
3 cups drained crushed pineapple	¾ cup drained crushed pineapple

A small vanilla recipe from pages 24 through 35

Add pineapple to ice cream when it is frozen but still soft.

MOCHA ALMOND FUDGE

Gallon	Quart
6 T. instant coffee	1 ½ T. instant coffee
2 ½ cups chopped toasted almonds	½ cup chopped toasted almonds
1 large can chocolate sauce	¼ large can chocolate sauce

A small vanilla recipe from pages 24 through 35

Dissolve instant coffee in warm mixture in ice cream recipe. Add nuts when ice cream is partially frozen. Marble chocolate sauce through ice cream after it is frozen. This is easier to do as you transfer the ice cream from the canister to another container.

ALMOND ICE CREAM

Gallon

2 cups chopped almonds
1 T. almond extract

Quart

½ cup chopped almonds
¼ T. almond extract

A small vanilla recipe from pages 24 through 35

Almonds may be toasted or not, as desired. Substitute almond extract for one tablespoon vanilla extract in ice cream mixture. Add nuts when ice cream is partially frozen.

MARBLE FUDGE ICE CREAM

Gallon

Quart

1 large can chocolate sauce   ¼ large can chocolate sauce

A large vanilla recipe from pages 24 through 35

Marble chocolate sauce through ice cream after it is frozen. This is easier to do as you transfer ice cream from the canister to another container.

BANANA ICE CREAM

Gallon	Quart
6 ripe bananas	1 ½ ripe bananas
A small vanilla recipe from pages 24 through 35	

Mash bananas well. Omit half of vanilla called for in ice cream recipe. Add mashed bananas to ice cream mixture before freezing.

For Banana Nut Ice Cream, add 2 cups chopped almonds, pecans or walnuts when ice cream is partially frozen.

BUTTER PECAN ICE CREAM

Gallon	Quart
1 ½ cups chopped pecans	⅓ cup chopped pecans
3 T. butter	1 T. butter
Brown sugar	Brown sugar

A small vanilla recipe from pages 24 through 35

Saute nuts in butter over low heat about 5 minutes. Cool. Substitute brown sugar for sugar called for in ice cream recipe. Add nuts when ice cream is partially frozen.

MAPLE ICE CREAM

Gallon   Quart

2 T. maple flavoring   ½ T. maple flavoring

A large vanilla recipe from pages 24 through 35

Substitute maple flavoring for half of the vanilla in the ice cream recipe.

For Maple Nut Ice Cream, add ½ cup chopped nuts for quart (2 cups for gallon) when ice cream is partially frozen.

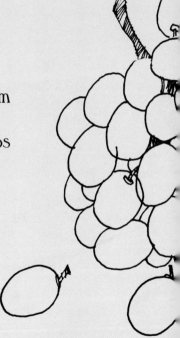

GRAPE ICE CREAM

Gallon	Quart
1 ½ cans (6 ounce size) frozen grape juice concentrate	⅓ can (6 ounce size) frozen grape juice concentrate
4 T. lemon juice	1 T. lemon juice

A small vanilla recipe from pages 24 through 35

Thaw grape juice concentrate. Combine with lemon juice. Add to ice cream mixture before freezing.

CHOCOLATE CHIP ICE CREAM

Gallon	Quart
1 bag (12 ounces) miniature semi-sweet chocolate chips	¼ bag (12 ounces) miniature semi-sweet chocolate chips

A small vanilla recipe from pages 24 through 35

Add miniature chips to ice cream after it is frozen but still soft. For mocha chip ice cream, add chocolate chips to recipe on page 42.

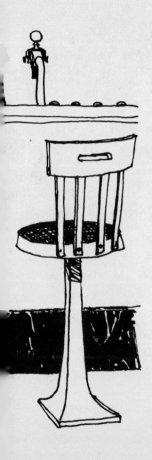

TOASTED COCONUT ICE CREAM

Gallon	Quart
4 cups shredded coconut	1 cup shredded coconut
1 T. coconut flavoring	¼ T. coconut flavoring
(optional)	(optional)

A small vanilla recipe from pages 24 through 35

Spread coconut in shallow pan. Toast in 350° oven about 15 minutes, stirring occasionally. Substitute coconut flavoring for 1 tablespoon vanilla in ice cream recipe. Add coconut to ice cream when partially frozen.

HELPFUL HINTS

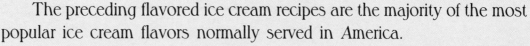

The preceding flavored ice cream recipes are the majority of the most popular ice cream flavors normally served in America.

If you would like to make other flavors do not be afraid to try. Here are some hints that may help you. Any fruit may be substituted for the fruits used in the preceding recipes. Just remember to add additional sugar if the fruit needs sweetening. Use the extra space provided in most recipes to change amounts of flavoring to correspond to your own taste buds. For example, after making chocolate ice cream for the first time, you may feel it needs more or less chocolate or sugar. After all, one advantage to making your own ice cream is that you can make it the way you like it.

Try making several flavors at one time. For example, when your vanilla is finished, place it in one-quart freezer containers. Spoon chocolate sauce through one quart for Marble Fudge Ice Cream (page 65), and strawberries through one quart for Strawberries and Cream Ice Cream (page 38).

SHERBET

Sherbet is basically a frozen dessert which is made with a fruit juice or puree, a sweetener, and water. Beaten egg white, milk, gelatine or marshmallows are added to this, and this is what makes the difference between sherbet and ices. It gives sherbet a richer, more creamy taste.

Sherbet was originally a French creation made up of fruit juices frozen with liqueurs or wines. Portions were scooped out and sprinkled with more of the same liqueur or wine.

Sherbet is also applied occasionally to describe a sweet fruit drink or a fizzy drink made from sodium bicarbonate, sugar, and tartaric acid.

Because several of the sherbet recipes which follow use egg whites, which are often left over after making custard ice cream, you might consider making one gallon of ice cream and one gallon of sherbet on the same day. You can use the same ice and salt mix for both.

LEMON MILK SHERBET

Gallon	Quart
6 egg whites	1 ½ egg whites
¾ cup sugar	¼ cup sugar
3 cups light corn syrup	¾ cup light corn syrup
6 cups whole milk	1 ½ cups whole milk
3 t. grated lemon rind	1 t. grated lemon rind
2 cups lemon juice	½ cup lemon juice

Beat egg whites until stiff, but not dry. Gradually beat in sugar, then corn syrup, milk, lemon rind and juice. Chill before putting into canister to freeze.

This is a good way to use some of your egg whites left over from other recipes.

LIME MILK SHERBET

Gallon	Quart
6 egg whites	2 egg whites
¾ cup sugar	¼ cup sugar
3 cups light corn syrup	¾ cup light corn syrup
6 cups whole milk	1 ½ cups whole milk
3 t. grated lemon rind	1 t. grated lemon rind
2 cups lime juice	½ cup lime juice

Beat egg whites until stiff, but not dry. Gradually beat in sugar, then corn syrup, milk, lime rind and juice. Chill and freeze.

ORANGE MILK SHERBET

Gallon	Quart
6 egg whites	1 ½ egg whites
¾ cup sugar	¼ cup sugar
3 cups light corn syrup	¾ cup light corn syrup
6 cups whole milk	1 ½ cups whole milk
3 t. grated orange rind	1 t. grated orange rind
2 cups orange juice	½ cup orange juice

Beat egg whites until stiff, but not dry. Gradually beat in sugar, then corn syrup, milk, orange rind and juice. Chill and freeze.

STRAWBERRY SHERBET

Gallon	Quart
4 cups water	1 cup water
1 ½ cups sugar	⅓ cup sugar
2 quarts fresh strawberries	½ quart fresh strawberries
½ cup lemon juice	⅛ cup lemon juice
2 packages gelatin	½ package gelatin
4 egg whites	1 egg white

Mix sugar and water together and boil for about five minutes or until the consistency of light syrup. Pour ¼ cup of cold water in a bowl and dissolve gelatin in it. Add gelatin to hot syrup. Press berries through a sieve and add lemon juice. Add to syrup mixture. Chill. Beat egg whites stiff, add to chilled mixture and freeze.

ORANGE CREAM SHERBET

Quart		Gallon	Quart		Gallon
¼	cup cold water	1	¾	cups orange juice	3
1	cups sugar	4	¼	t. salt	½
¾	cups hot water	3	1	cups cream	4
	rind from 4 oranges		½	envelopes powdered gelatin	2
½	cups lemon juice	2	1	eggs	4

Grate the orange rind and set aside. Pour the cold water into a bowl and sprinkle the gelatine on top. Add half of the sugar and the hot water and stir until dissolved. Then add the orange rind and orange and lemon juices and chill. Freeze until mushy, and set aside. Beat the cream until stiff and add the rest of the sugar and salt. Separate the egg whites from the yolks and beat until stiff. Beat the yolks until thick and lemon colored. Then add both to the cream. Mix with frozen mixture and continue freezing.

This cream sherbet makes a rich dessert.

ORANGE-LEMON SHERBET

Gallon	Quart
4 ½ cups sugar	1 ¼ cups sugar
1 ½ cups orange juice	⅓ cup orange juice
10 cups milk	2 ½ cups milk
¾ cup lemon juice	¼ cup lemon juice
½ t. salt	¼ t. salt
2 envelopes powdered gelatine	½ envelopes powdered gelatine

Peel orange and lemon and grate rinds. Squeeze out juice and mix with salt and sugar. Pour a small amount of the milk out into a bowl and sprinkle the gelatine on top. Stir thoroughly and then heat over a double boiler until gelatine dissolves. Then add to the rest of the milk and place in the canister of the freezer.

PINEAPPLE MILK SHERBET

Gallon	Quart
2 cups unsweetened pineapple juice	½ cup unsweetened pineapple juice
2 t. grated lemon rind	½ t. grated lemon rind
9 T. lemon juice	2 T. lemon juice
2 cups sugar	½ cup sugar
¼ t. salt	¼ t. salt
8 cups cold milk	2 cups cold milk

Stir all the above ingredients together in the milk. Freeze.

PEACH SHERBET

Gallon	Quart
2 cups water	½ cup water
3 cups sugar	¾ cup sugar
4 cups fresh peach pulp	1 cup fresh peach pulp
2 cups fresh orange juice	¼ cup fresh orange juice
1 cup fresh lemon juice	¼ cup fresh lemon juice
2 egg whites	½ egg white
¼ t. salt	¼ t. salt

Peel and pit peaches and force through a fine sieve. This will give you the pulp. Boil the sugar and water for 5 minutes. Then mix all the ingredients together and freeze.

GRAPE SHERBET

Gallon	Quart
2 cups cold water	½ cup cold water
6 cups boiling water	1½ cups boiling water
4 cups sugar	1 cup sugar
9 T. lemon juice	2 T. lemon juice
2 cans frozen grape juice concentrate	½ can frozen grape juice concentrate
1 cup orange juice	¼ cup orange juice
1 t. salt	¼ t. salt
2 envelopes gelatine	½ envelope gelatine

Boil the sugar and hot water together for about 5 minutes — until the consistency of light syrup. Pour cold water in a bowl and sprinkle gelatine on top. Combine with syrup and stir until dissolved. Cool slightly and then add the remaining ingredients. Freeze.

RASPBERRY SHERBET

Gallon	Quart
4 cups water	1 cup water
1 ½ cups sugar	⅓ cup sugar
2 quarts fresh raspberries	½ quart fresh raspberries
9 T. lemon juice	2 T. lemon juice
2 packages gelatine	½ package gelatine
4 egg whites	1 egg white

Mix the sugar and water together and boil for about 5 minutes until the consistency of syrup. Pour ¼ cup of the water into a bowl and sprinkle the gelatine on top. Stir until completely dissolved. Then add to the hot syrup. Press raspberries through a sieve and add lemon juice. Add to syrup mixture. Chill. Beat until stiff, but not dry and add the egg whites. Freeze.

STRAWBERRY PINEAPPLE SHERBET

Gallon
¾ cup cold water

2½ cups sugar

3 pints fresh strawberries

7½ cups (3 1-pound, 4 ounce cans) pineapple juice

½ t. salt

3 egg whites

2 packages gelatine

Quart
¼ cup cold water

⅔ cup sugar

1 pint fresh strawberries

2 cups pineapple juice

¼ t. salt

1 egg white

½ package gelatine

Pour water into a bowl and sprinkle gelatine on top. Let stand for 5 minutes. Mix pineapple juice and sugar together and heat until boiling, then stir in the gelatine and chill. Wash the berries, then drain them, mash, and force through a fine sieve. Combine with pineapple mixture, into canister and partially freeze. Pour into bowl and beat until fluffy. Beat the egg white until stiff and add the salt. Fold this mixture into the sherbet, return to tray and continue freezing until firm.

LEMON-LIME SHERBET

Gallon

4 cups milk
4 cups light cream
½ t. salt
9 T. sugar
1 ½ cups (2 6-ounce cans) frozen
lemon-and-limeade, undiluted
1 envelope gelatine

Quart

1 cup milk
1 cup light cream
¼ t. salt
2 T. sugar
½ cup frozen
lemon-and-limeade, undiluted
½ envelope gelatine

Pour ½ cup of the milk in a small saucepan and sprinkle gelatine on top. Let stand for 5 minutes. Dissolve over very low heat and mix with remaining ingredients. Chill and then freeze.

GRAPEFRUIT SHERBET

Gallon	Quart
3 cups sugar	¾ cup sugar
4½ cups water	1⅛ cups water
¾ cup lemon juice	¼ cup lemon juice
6 cups fresh grapefruit juice	1½ cups fresh grapefruit juice
1 cup orange juice	¼ cup orange juice
½ t. salt	¼ t. salt
6 egg whites	2 egg whites
2 packages gelatine	½ package gelatine

Put ½ cup of the water in a bowl and add gelatine — stir until dissolved. Boil the sugar and water for about 10 minutes — until the consistency of syrup. Add the gelatine to the syrup, and chill. Then mix in the lemon, grapefruit, and orange juices and salt. Beat the egg whites until stiff and add to grapefruit mixture, and freeze.

HOMEMADE TOPPINGS

A great favorite with young and old alike is the ice cream sundae. The ice cream parlor with its infinite variety of fancy sundaes which were not only delicious, but were often artistic works are not as common today as they were years ago. However, attractive and delicious sundaes can be made at home and are one of the most appealing desserts that a good host or hostess can serve to guests. The following sundae topping recipes are just a few examples of what can be done. This is an area in which you should let your imagination go to work for you. Don't hesitate to try anything once.

A real treat for a party of youngsters or adults is to put a large variety of sauces and toppings, nuts, cherries and fruits in bowls, along with a big bowl of ice cream, and let all of the guests make their own concoctions.

We have divided the topping section into two parts. First comes home made toppings requiring cooking. These are followed by an easy topping section.

91

VANILLA SAUCE

½ cup sugar
1 T. cornstarch
1 cup boiling water
2 T. butter
1 t. vanilla extract
dash of salt

Mix the sugar and cornstarch together in a small saucepan. Stir in the boiling water and simmer for 5 minutes. Stir in the butter and vanilla extract and add salt. Mix well and serve warm. Makes 1 ¼ cups of sauce.

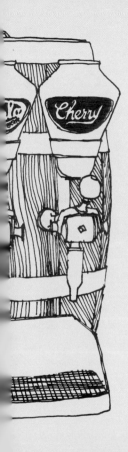

BUTTER SAUCE

½ cup butter
1 cup sugar
½ cup light cream

Mix all ingredients together and cook until sugar is completely dissolved, stirring constantly. Serve warm.

BROWN SUGAR SAUCE

⅓ cup butter or margarine
½ cup heavy cream
2 cups firmly packed light brown sugar
¼ t. salt
⅓ cup light corn syrup

Mix all the ingredients together in a saucepan and bring to boil. Cook rapidly for 3 minutes (220° F. on a candy thermometer). Serve warm over ice cream.

FOAMY SAUCE

1 cup confectioner's (powdered) sugar
½ cup soft butter or margarine
2 eggs
1 T. brandy or rum

Separate the egg yolks from the whites and beat separately. Over a double boiler cream the sugar and butter together. Add in the egg yolks and cook over simmering water. Stir constantly until thickened. Fold in the egg whites and brandy or rum. Serve warm. Serves 4 to 6.

HONEY-CREAM SAUCE

½ cup honey
½ cup light cream
2 T. butter
rum flavoring

Mix together the honey, cream, and butter and cook over low heat for about 10 minutes. Add a little rum flavoring if desired. Makes about 1 cup. Serve warm.

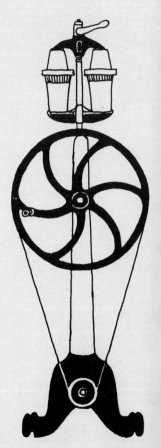

TAFFY SUNDAE SAUCE

¾ cup butter or margarine
¾ cup molasses
¾ cup sugar
¾ cup diluted evaporated milk
1 ½ t. vanilla extract
1 cup pecans

Melt the butter over a very low heat and add in the sugar and molasses. Bring all to a rapid boil then reduce the heat and boil for 2 minutes, stirring constantly to prevent burning. Remove from heat and cool slightly. Stir in the remaining ingredients. Serve hot or cold over your favorite vanilla ice cream. Makes about 2½ cups.

MARSHMALLOW SAUCE

½ lb. marshmallows
½ cup orange juice
1 T. maraschino juice
2 cups sugar
⅔ cup water
3 egg whites

Mix the orange juice and maraschino together. Cut the marshmallows into small pieces and soak in the orange juice mixture. Combine the sugar and water and cook until the consistency of syrup. Then beat the egg whites and pour the syrup slowly on top. Beat until creamy, and cool. When cooled, add the marshmallows.

CUSTARD SAUCE

1 ½ cups milk
3 egg yolks
3 T. sugar
⅛ t. salt
vanilla or almond extract

Heat the milk to boiling point in a double boiler over simmering water. Mix together the egg yolks, sugar, and salt. Stir in a small amount of hot milk then return all to the remaining milk in the double boiler. Cook, stirring constantly, until thickened. Cool. Flavor sauce with vanilla or almond extract. A little lemon rind may also be added if desired. Makes about 1 ¾ cups.

CHOCOLATE CUSTARD SAUCE

4 egg yolks, slightly beaten
¼ cup sugar
⅛ t. salt
2 oz. (2 squares) unsweetened chocolate
2 cups milk
½ t. vanilla extract

Add the sugar and salt to the beaten egg yolks and mix together well. Melt the chocolate in the milk, stirring constantly, then beat to blend. Stir this into the egg mixture. Cook in a double boiler over simmering water, stirring constantly, until the mixture thickens. Add the vanilla, cool, and chill. Makes about 2½ cups.

CHOCOLATE SAUCE

2 oz. (2 squares) unsweetened chocolate
¾ cup milk
1½ cups sugar
3 T. light corn syrup
¼ t. salt
2 T. butter
1 t. vanilla extract

Melt the chocolate in the milk in a saucepan over very low heat. Stir constantly. When chocolate is completely melted and blended in, beat until smooth. Add the sugar, corn syrup and salt. Cook for 2 or 3 minutes, stirring occasionally. Add the butter and vanilla. Makes 2 cups.

BITTERSWEET-CHOCOLATE SAUCE

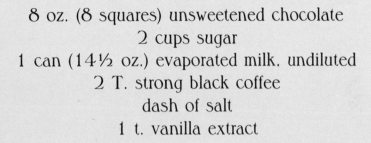

8 oz. (8 squares) unsweetened chocolate
2 cups sugar
1 can (14½ oz.) evaporated milk, undiluted
2 T. strong black coffee
dash of salt
1 t. vanilla extract

Melt the chocolate in a double boiler over boiling water. Add in the sugar and blend well. Cook, covered, over boiling water for 30 minutes. Add the evaporated milk, coffee, salt and vanilla and beat until smooth and thick. This sauce should be served hot. It can be made ahead of time and kept in the refrigerator for several weeks. To reheat, simply put in the double boiler over boiling water. Makes about 3 cups.

HOT CARAMEL SAUCE

1 ½ cups sugar
½ cup light corn syrup
6 T. butter
1 cup light cream
½ t. salt
½ t. vanilla extract

Mix together in a saucepan the sugar, corn syrup, 3 tablespoons of the butter, and ½ cup of the cream. Bring to a boil and gradually add the remaining butter and cream. Cook over medium heat, stirring occasionally, until thickened. Remove from heat and add the salt and vanilla. Serve warm. To reheat, simply put sauce in a double boiler over simmering water. Makes 1 ¾ cups.

HOT FUDGE SAUCE

1 cup sugar
2 T. flour
½ t. salt
1 cup water
2 oz. (2 squares) unsweetened chocolate
2 T. butter
1 t. vanilla extract

Combine the sugar, flour, and salt in a saucepan and blend in the water. Add the chocolate and cook over medium heat, stirring constantly until the mixture boils. Remove from the heat and blend in the butter and vanilla extract. Serve hot over creamy vanilla ice cream.

BUTTERSCOTCH SAUCE

½ cup light corn syrup
⅓ cup butter or margarine
1 ½ cups firmly packed brown sugar
⅔ cup light cream

Combine the corn syrup, butter, and brown sugar in a saucepan and cook, stirring occasionally, over medium heat until thickened. Cool for about 5 minutes then blend in the cream. Serve hot or cold. Makes 2¼ cups.

NUT-FUDGE SAUCE

2 cups sugar
1 cup brown sugar
3 oz. (3 squares) unsweetened chocolate
¾ cup cream
2 T. butter
1 t. vanilla
1 cup chopped nuts

Mix together in a saucepan the sugar, brown sugar, chocolate, cream, and butter. Cook over medium heat until the mixture crinkles around the edge of the saucepan. Remove from the heat and add the vanilla and chopped nuts. Serve at once.

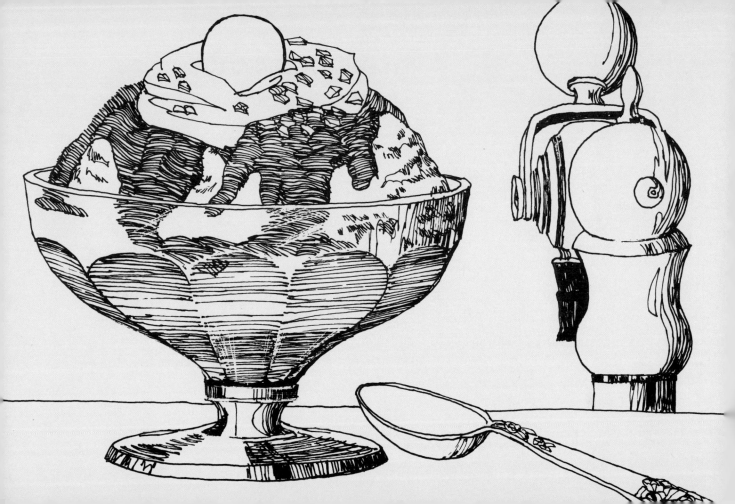

EASY SUNDAES

On the pages that follow are recipes for quick and easy sundaes that you can make in a few minutes with foodstuffs that are readily available in your kitchen or nearby store.

Don't limit yourself to vanilla ice cream when making sundaes. Try these toppings with several different kinds of ice cream, and don't hesitate to use two types of ice creams with two different toppings.

One last word, don't forget the whipped cream, chopped nuts and cherry to top off your sundaes. They add the crowning touch to your home made creations.

EASY SUNDAES

ORANGE-BLUEBERRY SUNDAE

Garnish two scoops of peach ice cream with equal amounts of orange segments, sliced bananas, and blueberries.

STOP-AND-GO SUNDAE

Combine chopped green and red maraschino cherries and add a little light corn syrup. Pour over vanilla or cherry ice cream.

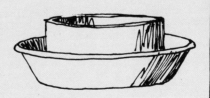

EASY SUNDAES

HOT CARAMEL SUNDAE

Add 2 T. water to ½ lb. of caramels and melt down to a thick syrup over hot water. Top with nuts if desired.

ORIENTAL SUNDAE

Cut up into small pieces a couple of undrained preserved kumquats. Spoon over chocolate ice cream.

PEACH SUNDAE

Slice up frozen or sweetened fresh peaches and serve over rich French Vanilla ice cream.

EASY SUNDAES

PINK SUNDAE

Spoon 1 or 2 T. grenadine over vanilla ice cream — top with a sprig of mint.

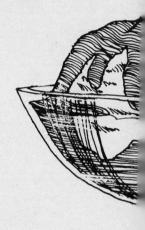

PINEAPPLE SUNDAE

Spoon some canned crushed pineapple over vanilla or banana ice cream, include a little juice as well.

TART ORANGE SUNDAE

Pour canned frozen orange juice concentrate over chocolate or vanilla ice cream.

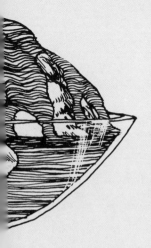

EASY SUNDAES

PARTY ORANGE SUNDAE

3 very large oranges
1 cup strawberries
1 banana
1 pint orange sherbet

Cut the oranges in half and neatly scoop out the orange segments. Slice the banana and combine with the strawberries and orange segments. Place a scoop of sherbet in each orange shell and top with the fruit. Serve immediately. Serves 6. Grapefruit can be substituted for the orange if desired.

MARSHMALLOW SUNDAE

You can either buy ready-made marshmallow cream or make your own by melting down marshmallows slowly in a double boiler. Best on chocolate, peach, and pineapple ice creams.

EASY SUNDAES

MOLASSES CHIP SUNDAE

Sprinkle some crushed molasses chips over vanilla, chocolate, or banana ice cream.

MOCHA SUNDAE

Mix powdered instant coffee with your favorite chocolate syrup and pour over chocolate or vanilla or coffee ice cream.

MINCEMEAT SUNDAE

Mix a little rum or brandy in with the mincemeat. Serve warm over ice cream — great at Christmas time.

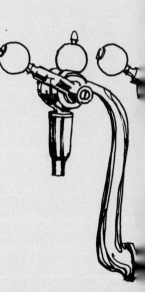

EASY SUNDAES

RUM-MANGO SUNDAE

1 large ripe mango
⅓ cup rum
¼ cup sugar
vanilla ice cream

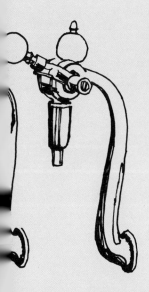

Peel the mango and slice it into thin slices (about ¼ inch). Put into a shallow dish and sprinkle the sugar and rum on top. Refrigerate for 1 hour before serving. When chilled and ready to serve, spoon over vanilla or mango ice cream. Serves 4.

JAM SUNDAE

Serve your favorite jam over ice cream. Cherry, plum, apricot, and any berry jams are delicious.

EASY SUNDAES

MAPLE-RUM SUNDAE

Heat up as much maple syrup as you will use in a double boiler. Flavor it with a little rum or rum extract and serve over coffee or your favorite nut ice cream.

GINGER SUNDAE

Pour ginger marmalade or chopped preserved ginger root in syrup over vanilla ice cream.

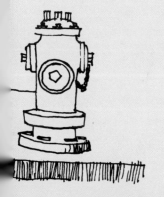

MARMALADE SUNDAE

Top vanilla ice cream with your favorite marmalade.

EASY SUNDAES

CANDIED FRUIT SUNDAE
Spoon moist mixed candied fruits over vanilla or pistachio ice cream.

DESERT SUNDAE
Moisten chopped fresh dates with honey and serve over butter-pecan or burnt-almond ice cream.

TROPICAL SUNDAE
Combine chopped coconut, white raisins, and chopped walnuts to butterscotch sauce and pour over ice cream.

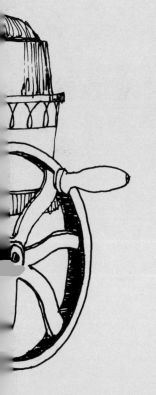

EASY SUNDAES

BRANDIED FRUIT SUNDAE

Cut up a quantity of brandied fruit and serve over coffee, pineapple, coconut, banana, or vanilla ice cream.

COOKIE SUNDAE

Top your favorite ice cream with crushed fig cookies, coconut bars, or macaroons.

PEANUT BRITTLE SUNDAE

Sprinkle crushed peanut brittle over vanilla, chocolate, coffee, or caramel ice cream.

EASY SUNDAES

LIQUEUR SUNDAE

Top your favorite ice cream with Cointreau, creme de menthe, or any liqueur.

PINEAPPLE-GINGER SUNDAE

Mix in a small amount of chopped candied ginger root to pineapple jam and serve over vanilla ice cream.

CHOCOLATE-RUM SUNDAE

Melt down chocolate rum wafers in a double boiler over hot water and serve over vanilla or chocolate ice cream.

EASY SUNDAES

BLACK AND WHITE SUNDAE

Use one scoop of vanilla ice cream and one scoop of chocolate. Cover the chocolate with marshmallow sauce and vanilla with chocolate sauce. Add whipped cream, cherries and nuts.

COCONUT SUNDAE

Roll balls of your favorite ice cream in shredded coconut and top with your favorite sauce.

EASY SUNDAES

FLAVORED WHIPPED CREAM TOPPINGS

1 ½ cups heavy cream
½ cup sugar
⅛ t. salt
½ t. vanilla extract

Before whipping, add one of the following to the basic recipe above to make a delicious thick, creamy topping. Instant coffee powder, instant cocoa mix, brown sugar instead of granulated sugar, quick strawberry-flavored beverage mix, any flavoring extract.

Or, one of the following can be folded into the whipped cream. Chopped nuts, macaroon crumbs, chocolate sprinkles, chopped raisins, or grenadine instead of sugar.

BANANA SPLIT

One ripe banana
1 scoop each of vanilla, chocolate, and strawberry ice cream
2 T. strawberry preserves
2 T. of pineapple preserves
2 T. of chocolate sauce
Whipped cream
2 T. of chopped nuts
1 maraschino cherry

Split the banana into halves lengthwise. Arrange ice cream scoops in a row between banana halves. Spoon strawberry preserves over one scoop, pineapple over another and chocolate sauce over the last. Top with whipped cream and garnish with nuts and cherry.

OTHER CONCOCTIONS

The ways in which ice cream can be used for delightful desserts and snacks is probably infinite.

On the pages which follow, we cover many of the more popular ice cream concoctions in use today.

If you keep the ingredients on hand, and if you always have your own delicious home made ice cream in the freezer, you can serve super desserts that will be the delight of your family and guests with very little effort on your part . . . and when you use the rich custard and cream varieties of ice cream, you'll be creating desserts which will rival those served to royalty.

ICE CREAM SODAS

Sodas are easy to make. First take a small amount of vanilla ice cream and blend it thoroughly with the syrup in the bottom of the glass before adding the carbonated water. This way, you are first creating a flavored soda water. Then add a large scoop of vanilla ice cream. Top with whipped cream and a cherry.

For more flavorful sodas try using flavored ice creams. For example, use strawberry ice cream in strawberry sodas, banana ice cream in banana sodas and so on. Just remember to first mix some of the ice cream with the syrup to create the base.

FLOATS

Floats are made with flavored soda water and vanilla ice cream. All you have to do is fill a large glass with root beer, cola, or any other flavored soda water and then add a large scoop of vanilla ice cream. The root beer float is the all-time favorite.

FREEZES

The freeze is a sherbet soda. First mix a small amount of sherbet with the syrup in the bottom of the glass. Use lemon, lime, or orange syrup with the same flavor of sherbet. Then add carbonated water and top off with a large scoop of sherbet. You can stop there if you wish, or you can carefully spoon additional sherbet around the top of the glass and top it off with whipped cream and a cherry. This is a wonderful thirst quencher for a hot day.

MILK SHAKES AND MALTS

If you like thin milk shakes, you can use an egg beater, blender or electric mixer. Simply place ½ cup milk, 2 scoops of ice cream, and your favorite syrup in any of the above and mix. For malts, add 1 tablespoon malted milk. You will soon have a conventional shake.

If you like thick milk shakes, you can't use an egg beater or electric mixer. You must use a blender or a milk shake mixer. Use the same proportions as above and then keep adding ice cream until it is thick enough to suit you.

The home made ice cream milk shake is so good that you'll never want any other kind.

FROSTEDS

Frosteds are super sodas. First mix syrup with a small amount of ice cream and then add soda water to fill the glass. Carefully spoon several spoonfuls of the same flavor of ice cream as the syrup around the top of the glass to make a cover for the glass. Then spoon vanilla ice cream on top of it and finish it off with whipped cream and a cherry. What you have done is covered the soda. It is frosted.

KAREN'S ORANGE FREEZE

¾ cup freshly squeezed orange juice, or frozen orange juice
1 T. lemon juice
6 or 7 scoops of orange sherbet

Put all the ingredients in the blender. Blend until almost smooth but still thick. Pour into tall glasses and top with a cherry. Makes 2 average sized servings.

MERINGUE ICE CREAM CUPS

1 egg white
⅓ cup sugar
½ t. vanilla
⅓ cup chopped pecans
3 soda crackers, crushed

Beat the egg white in a mixing bowl until soft peaks form. Add the sugar and vanilla gradually until stiff peaks form. Stir in the pecans and crackers. Spread a rounded teaspoonful of the mixture on the bottom and sides of 6 well-buttered muffin cups. Bake at 325° for 25 to 30 minutes until light golden brown. Cool about 5 minutes. To remove from the cups, carefully loosen the edges with a paring knife.

These cups, when cooled, can be filled with any combination of ice cream, syrup, or fresh fruit, etc.

CHERRIES JUBILEE

2 T. butter

2 T. sugar

1 t. grated orange rind

1 t. grated lemon rind

¼ cup orange juice

¼ cup lemon juice

¼ cup Kirsch

3 cups canned bing cherries, pitted and drained

¼ cup warm brandy

In a chafing dish melt the butter over high heat. Blend in the sugar, mix well, and heat until the mixture bubbles. Stir in orange and lemon rinds and simmer until the mixture is light brown. Stir in orange and lemon juices and cook until mixture bubbles again. Add Kirsch and cherries. Stir until the cherries are well saturated. Pour in the warm brandy, light it, and stir the sauce until the flames die away. Serve over vanilla ice cream.

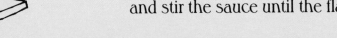

BAKED ALASKA

1 cup sifted all-purpose flour
⅔ cup sugar
¼ cup shortening
½ cup milk
1 ½ t. baking powder

½ t. salt
1 t. vanilla extract
1 egg
1 quart brick ice cream
meringue

Grease and flour lightly a 9-inch square pan. Sift together the flour, sugar, baking powder and salt in a mixing bowl. Add the shortening and milk. Beat 1 ½ minutes with a mixer on low speed or 225 strokes by hand. Add in the egg and vanilla and beat for another 1 ½ minutes. Pour into pan and bake at 350° for 20 to 25 minutes, or until a toothpick inserted into cake comes out clean. Cool. Place cake on a cookie sheet and cut strips 2 inches wide from each side of cake. Put ice cream on top of cake and completely cover both with meringue. Seal meringue to edges. Bake at 450° for 5 minutes, or until lightly browned. Serve at once.

MERINGUE TOPPING

8 egg whites at room temperature
pinch of salt
¾ cup superfine sugar

Beat the egg whites and salt until they form soft peaks. Still beating, slowly pour in the sugar and continue to beat for about 5 minutes, until the egg whites are stiff and glossy. Immediately spread over cake and ice cream.

ICE CREAM BONBONS

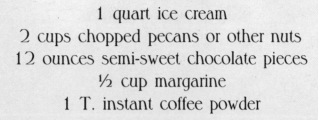

1 quart ice cream
2 cups chopped pecans or other nuts
12 ounces semi-sweet chocolate pieces
½ cup margarine
1 T. instant coffee powder

Make your ice cream balls with a large melon ball scoop. Roll each ball in nuts immediately and put in freezer until completely frozen, at least 1 hour. Melt the chocolate and margarine in a double boiler over hot water. Mix in the coffee. Take away from heat but keep warm over hot water. Using a fork, dip the ice cream balls into the chocolate-coffee mixture, working as quickly as possible. Dip sets of 10 or 12 at a time, then return to freezer and continue. When the chocolate is set completely, put the bonbons in paper cups, 3 or 4 to a serving. Cover or wrap with foil or plastic wrap and store in your freezer until ready to serve. Makes 30 to 36 bonbons.

PARFAIT

Parfait is a French word meaning "perfect." A phrase used by many to describe this dish. American parfaits consist of ice cream served with whipped cream, fruit, or other sauces piled in layers in a tall, narrow glass called a "parfait glass." It is often topped with sweet whipped cream and garnished with a maraschino cherry.

In a parfait glass or juice glass, alternate layers of ice cream with jam, syrup, baby or junior fruit, or marshmallow cream. Here are some good combinations you can use:

- Strawberry ice cream and strawberry jam
- Vanilla ice cream and red raspberry jam
- Cherry ice cream and almond-flavored whipped cream

PARFAIT

- Vanilla ice cream with apricot and apple, or pear and pineapple .baby or junior fruit
- Chocolate ice cream and marshmallow cream

Any combination of ice cream and sauce that strikes your fancy can be tried, and can't help but be delicious!

PRINCE PUCKLER'S BOMBE

3 T. rum
2 cups coarsely crushed macaroons
1 quart chocolate ice cream
1 pint vanilla ice cream
1 pint strawberry ice cream or raspberry sherbet
1 cup heavy cream, whipped, sweetened, and
flavored with vanilla extract
fresh strawberries or shaved chocolate

Chill a 6-cup fluted bombe mold for 1 hour. Sprinkle rum over macaroon crumbs. Stir and let stand about one hour. Soften the chocolate ice cream slightly — until it can be pressed into the mold. Do not let it melt into a liquid. Pack firmly into the bottom of the mold and well into the sides. Sprinkle with a layer of ⅓ of the macaroon crumbs. Cover the mold and freeze until the crumbs and ice cream are hard. Let the vanilla

PRINCE PUCKLER'S BOMBE

ice cream soften and pack it into the mold, top with half of the remaining crumbs. Cover the mold and freeze again. Repeat with the strawberry ice cream and the rest of the crumbs. Cover the mold and freeze for 6 to 8 hours or until the ice cream is very hard. Unmold and slice in long wedges to serve. Serve plain or garnish with whipped cream and fresh strawberries or shaved chocolate. Serves 12.

This spherical three-layered ice cream dessert was named after a noted Prussian cook and gourmet, Hermann von Puckler-Muskau.

BROWNIE ICE CREAM SANDWICHES

1 pint of your favorite ice cream, softened
1 package fudge brownie mix

Prepare and bake brownie mix as directed and cool. Cut through the center to make two halves. Spread ice cream between the layers and wrap in foil paper. Freeze until firm, about 2 to 3 hours. Remove from freezer a few minutes before serving. Cut into 1-inch slices and serve immediately. Refreeze unused slices. Makes 8 to 10 sandwiches.

INDEX

NOTES

NOTES

NOTES

NOTES

METRIC CONVERSION CHART

Liquid or Dry Measuring Cup (based on an 8 ounce cup)

1/4 cup = 60 ml
1/3 cup = 80 ml
1/2 cup = 125 ml
3/4 cup = 190 ml
1 cup = 250 ml
2 cups = 500 ml

Liquid or Dry Measuring Cup (based on a 10 ounce cup)

1/4 cup = 80 ml
1/3 cup = 100 ml
1/2 cup = 150 ml
3/4 cup = 230 ml
1 cup = 300 ml
2 cups = 600 ml

Liquid or Dry Teaspoon and Tablespoon

1/4 tsp. = 1.5 ml
1/2 tsp. = 3 ml
1 tsp. = 5 ml
3 tsp. = 1 tbs. = 15 ml

Temperatures

°F		°C
200	=	100
250	=	120
275	=	140
300	=	150
325	=	160
350	=	180
375	=	190
400	=	200
425	=	220
450	=	230
475	=	240
500	=	260
550	=	280

Pan Sizes (1 inch = 25 mm)

8-inch pan (round or square) = 200 mm x 200 mm
9-inch pan (round or square) = 225 mm x 225 mm
9 x 5 x 3-inch loaf pan = 225 mm x 125 mm x 75 mm
1/4 inch thickness = 5 mm
1/8 inch thickness = 2.5 mm

Pressure Cooker

100 Kpa = 15 pounds per square inch
70 Kpa = 10 pounds per square inch
35 Kpa = 5 pounds per square inch

Mass

1 ounce = 30 g
4 ounces = 1/4 pound = 125 g
8 ounces = 1/2 pound = 250 g
16 ounces = 1 pound = 500 g
2 pounds = 1 kg

Key (America uses an 8 ounce cup - Britain uses a 10 ounce cup)

ml = milliliter
l = liter
g = gram
K = Kilo (one thousand)
mm = millimeter
m = milli (a thousandth)
°F = degrees Fahrenheit

°C = degrees Celsius
tsp. = teaspoon
tbs. = tablespoon
Kpa = (pounds pressure per square inch)
This configuration is used for pressure cookers only.

Metric equivalents are rounded to conform to existing metric measuring utensils.